Australia's WILDLIFE

Australia's WILDLIFE

Text by Neil Hermes

AUSTRALIAN PICTURE LIBRARY

C&A CHILD & ASSOCIATES

AN ALL-AUSTRALIAN PUBLISHER

Front cover: Koala with young. (See page 9.)
Back cover: Echidna. (See page 23.)

Published by Child & Associates Publishing Pty Ltd
5 Skyline Place, Frenchs Forest, NSW,
Australia, 2086
A wholly owned Australian publishing company.
This book has been edited and designed in Australia
by the Publisher
Distributed by Gordon & Gotch Limited, Sydney

First edition 1988
Text by Neil Hermes
Captions by Dalys Newman
Photographs from the Australian Picture Library
© Australian Picture Library 1988
Printed in Hong Kong by South Sea International
Typesetting processed by Deblaere Typesetting Pty Ltd
Also published as part of *Australia: Land of Colour*

**National Library of Australia
Cataloguing-in-Publication**

Hermes, Neil.
    Australia's wildlife.

    ISBN 0 86777 164 X.

    1. Zoology – Australia. 2. Zoology – Australia
    – Pictorial works. I. Newman, Dalys. II. Australian
    Picture Library. III. Title.

591.994

Australia's Wildlife

In 1770 Captain James Cook tried to put into writing his amazement at the strange creatures he had encountered in the new continent that he was exploring:

> Besides the Animals, which I have before mentioned, called by the natives Kangaroo, or Kanguru, here are wolves [dingoes], Possums, an Animal like a ratt, and snakes, both of the Venemous and other sorts. Tame animals here are none except Dogs, and of these we never saw but one, who frequently came about our tents to pick up bones, etc. The Kangaroo are in the greatest number, for we seldom went into the country without seeing some.

And this was only just the beginning. It was about thirty years later that the platypus was discovered and this caused a scientific storm that lasted a century. At first, many of Australia's animals were believed to be hoaxes and this was especially so of the platypus. Once these strange creatures were accepted as real, the scientific battles began as to their relationship with other animals. There were carnivorous animals like cats that had pouches, huge bats that looked like foxes, poisonous snakes and fish that breathed air through lungs.

Of course many of the first reports of Australian wildlife appeared in the diaries of the Dutch explorers of the continent's northern and western coasts. The first written description of a kangaroo is attributed to William Dampier who, in 1699, landed at Shark Bay in Western Australia. He wrote:

> The Land-Animals that we saw here were only a sort of Racoons, different from those of the West Indies, chiefly as to their legs; for these have very short fore-legs; but go jumping upon them as the others do (and, like them, are very good meat).

This description is of one of the smallest of the kangaroo family, the banded hare-wallaby which is now restricted to two islands in Shark Bay.

The paradoxical platypus

The platypus probably caused most controversy when it appeared on the nineteenth-century scientific stage. The first animals were discovered in the Hawkesbury River, north of the infant Sydney colony in 1797. One of the discoverers wrote in his diary that he believed the creature to be a type of amphibious mole. One of the first scientists to examine a skin of a platypus called it 'paradoxus' based on the furry coat, duckbill and webbed feet. How justified he would have felt if he had known that this new little aquatic Australian also laid eggs and suckled its young with milk!

Once scientists accepted that the platypus did in fact exist, the debate as to where it fitted into the animal kingdom raged for decades. The platypus laid eggs but was warm blooded and so could not be a reptile. Since it had no feathers it was hardly a bird. But how could a furry warm-blooded mammal lay eggs? The issue was finally resolved when it was discovered that the platypus also produced milk for its young, even though the milk oozed from the female's body rather than coming from teats. The platypus was a mammal, albeit a very strange one.

The leathery bill of the platypus not only locates food but is highly sensitive to touch. In the murky waters where platypuses live, hearing and sight are senses which are of little value. In fact, platypuses close their ears and eyes when submerged. All information about location and feeding is sent to the animal's brain via the highly sensitive bill. Most of the diet consists of various insects and other aquatic invertebrates.

When not in the water, platypuses spend most of their time in short burrows located just above the water level. A separate, more complex burrow is built for nesting.

Two eggs are laid and the female incubates them by holding them against her body with her tail. The young hatch in a few weeks and then spend four or five months being fed milk from the numerous ducts on the female's body.

Although still found in most coastal districts of eastern Australia the platypus is considered to be vulnerable. There is a danger that the species is disappearing slowly as rivers are dammed and urban and industrial developments have their effects on the coastal rivers.

The other egg-laying mammal is the echidna. In fact there are two species of this extraordinary ant-eating specialist: one in Australia and the other in New Guinea. Echidnas are often incorrectly called anteaters or porcupines but this is quite misleading since they are certainly not related to either of these American or European animal groups.

Like the platypus, the echidna is a mammal; that is, it has warm blood, has hair and suckles its young on milk. Unlike the platypus, the echidna doesn't lay its egg in a nest. The egg is deposited in a pouch, similar to those of marsupials. How the echidna docs this is still not known. When the female lays the egg the body is probably doubled up and the egg laid directly into the pouch. The claws appear to be useless to help in this task. The egg then hatches in the pouch and the young is carried for as long as the poor mother can bear the spikes! The young is then left in a suitable hiding place until old enough to feed on its own.

The sluggish echidna has developed a fine protective coat made up of long pointed spines. These cover the whole upper surface of the body, although the underbelly is still only soft skin covered in hair. To protect this vulnerable area the echidna has developed two highly effective behavioural characteristics. The first is to roll completely into a ball. The head is tucked in with the tail and all that is exposed to the enemy is a ball of spikes. It is extraordinarily difficult to unroll an echidna that has wrapped itself up like this. The second escape route, and the one preferred by the echidna, is to dig into the ground a little way and only leave the spiky body exposed. Once an echidna has a grip on the ground it is again almost impossible to budge it.

These defence ploys mean that echidnas have few, if any, natural enemies, although dingoes and goannas may take the occasional echidna and Aborigines often collect them.

Echidnas are highly specialised in their eating habits. They live solely on ants and termites, or white ants. The Australian bush is full of the earth nest mounds of termites and these are often seen to have excavations on the surface. This is evidence of echidna activity. The echidna breaches the base of the mound with its strong front claws. The tongue is covered in a sticky saliva and this collects the milling termites. Like the platypus, the echidna has no teeth and the termites are ground up on the bony surface of the mouth.

Surprisingly, perhaps, echidnas are still widespread throughout the continent and although it is not particularly numerous there is no concern about its ability to survive.

The world's favourite Australian

It would be hard to separate the koala from kangaroos as Australia's most prominent ambassadors. Although it is the Flying Kangaroo that adorns the tail of Qantas aircraft it is the koala that stars in much of Australia's promotional tourist advertising overseas. Koalas have also been subjects of some international diplomacy with 'ambassadorial' animals sent to Japan and the United States in recent years. Unfortunately, some of these animals have died, which adds to the koala's chequered history since the time of European settlement.

Because of their nocturnal lifestyle, koalas spend the day asleep in the fork of a tree. This, together with their generally cuddly appearance, promotes the perception that koalas are docile and gentle animals. Nothing is further from the truth as many publicity-conscious politicians have discovered when cuddling a koala for the ever-present photographers. The sharp, strong claws are adapted for very agile climbing but can be put to other use!

Koalas are widespread on the eastern coast of Australia and are limited to places where their preferred food trees are found. Although the preference is eucalypts, and in particular river red gum, grey gum, swamp gum and blue gum, other types of trees are eaten at times. Koalas will drink water but they usually obtain all the water they need from their leafy diet.

There is evidence to suggest that koalas evolved from ground-dwelling animals, such as the modern wombat. How else can you explain the fact that koalas have downward-opening pouches and no tails, surely both disadvantageous to an inhabitant of the treetops. The koala is, however, remarkably well equipped for its gum leaf diet. The digestive system is unlike those of other mammals and can cope with the oils that gum leaves contain.

The story of the koala over the last two hundred years has been one of changing fortunes. When Europeans first arrived, koalas were widespread and common but kept in check by dingoes and Aborigines. As the Aborigines became more reliant on European food supplies and dingoes were shot, the koala population was suddenly able to expand unchecked. By the end of the last century, koala numbers were so high that a large fur trade was established. In 1924 the colossal number of two million koala skins were exported. In many areas uncontrolled shooting eliminated whole groups of koalas. As urban and agricultural development fragmented the forests into small pockets the remaining koalas suffered from other stresses. The preferred food trees died out under pressure from koalas, and dogs and cars took their toll. A small population of koalas survived in some northern suburbs of Sydney for many years until finally succumbing to a combination of these pressures.

Koalas now have a new threat. Although disease would have been a part of koala life in the past, for small populations of koalas under stress, disease is now of major concern. Fortunately a major credit card company has recently funded research into this problem in Australia and the Japanese are investing large amounts of money in studying the animals they have in their zoos.

Mention possums to most Australians and they immediately think of brush-tailed possums and the nuisance they can be when they use our houses as theirs. But the possums are a group of over twenty different animals.

The smallest possum is the little pygmy possum weighing less than 10 grams and small enough to sit on the palm of your hand. Its bigger cousin, the burramys or mountain pygmy possum, is one of the rarest mammals in Australia. Its story is interesting since it was first reported from fossils found in a cave. For over seventy years it was believed that this animal no longer existed until one turned up in a ski hut at Mount Hotham in Victoria. A small population is now also known to live near the summit of Mount Kosciusko. Burramys live beneath the snow in the winter, making tunnels in the buried vegetation. As the skiers are working hard at staying on their skis, burramys are busy staying alive in the snow beneath them. The survival of burramys within the ski fields depends on careful planning, especially concerning machine-packed ski runs and summertime activities.

The brush-tailed or common possum has a rather easier lot in life. Where it can it gets into the roofs of houses and plays havoc with the sleep of other residents. You see, possums are nocturnal and this is a large part of the problem. However, resolving to remove possums from your roof may be only the start of the problems. One unscrupulous entrepreneur offered to trap and remove possums from houses for a fee. The trapping worked well but the possum-catcher then released the villains into a nearby suburb where they took up new residences. The possum-catcher's services were then required again and the possums were returned near to their 'original homes'. The original complainants were assured that these were new possums moving into the vacated area and the cycle began again. Perhaps everyone was content. People were having possums removed from their homes, albeit for a short period, the possums were well travelled and well fed and no doubt the possum-catcher was happy!

Kangaroos are another group of Australian animals where the number of different species is often underestimated. More than fifty kinds are known and they are all restricted to Australia and New Guinea.

Continued on page 41 . . .

Gum leaves are the koala's main food and vast quantities need be eaten to supply the animal with its quota of nutrients. To cop with such dietary demands, the koala has an appendix about 2. metres long.

The koala usually gives birth to a single young which is carried on the mother's back after five to six months in the pouch. (Lor Pine Sanctuary, Brisbane.) (Previous page.)

The Aborigines named this cuddly-looking creature 'koala' meaning 'I don't drink' because the gum leaves it eats supply the moisture it needs. (Lone Pine Sanctuary, Brisbane.)

The koala's tail is replaced by a callused pad which enables it to sit for hours in the fork of a tree without discomfort.

Baby kangaroos—joeys—live in their mother's pouch until able to hop at her feet. Even then, when threatened with danger the joey will tumble quickly into the pouch for protection.

Boxing kangaroos. A very game fighter, the kangaroo uses his powerful buttress of a tail for support and kicks forward, striking with the nails of his two great toes.

Tree-kangaroos, members of the genus Dendrolagus. *These unusual marsupials found in north-eastern Queensland and New Guinea are well adapted to life above the ground.*

Red kangaroos—most widely known of Australia's marsupials. These kangaroos graze in mobs on the open plains and when in danger move at great speed, hopping on their hind feet with bounds as long as 8 metres.

As the dry season sets in across northern Australia wildlife becomes concentrated at the drying pools. ▲

Wallabies are usually found in hill or scrub country and apart from being smaller than the kangaroo they share the same characteristics. ▼

The charming little pademelons are mainly nocturnal, camping under logs and in thick vegetation during the day. (Bottom right.)

The yellow-footed rock-wallaby (Petrogale xanthopus)—an extremely acrobatic animal whose main home is the rocky ranges of northern and central South Australia. ►

16

Ring-tailed possums (Pseudocheirus peregrinus) have long prehensile tails, often carried rolled into a tight ring shape when not being used for climbing.

The lumbering wombat is an active burrower, sheltering in holes during the day and emerging at night to feed on grass, herbage and roots.▼

The sugar glider (Petaurus breviceps) *is probably the most abundant of Australia's 'flying' marsupials.They are tough, adaptable creatures with a widespread habitat.*

Ring-tailed possum. Australia has many varieties of pouched animals which live in trees and feed on honey, flowers or foliage. Although some species look similar to the American opossum they are not closely related and the correct name for the Australian variety is phalanger.

Once fairly common across much of mainland Australia, the western barred bandicoot
(Perameles bougainville) *is now reduced to a very few small colonies such as Bernier and
Dorre Islands in Shark Bay, Western Australia.*

The Top End rock rat (Zyzomys argurus).

Termite mounds in the Northern Territory. Northern Australian termites are the most primitive and largest in the world, being about 3 centimetres long. Their enormous homes are masterpieces of fantasy and sculpture, with structures often towering over 6 metres. They are built of earth particles joined together with saliva, and when dry they have the hardness of concrete.

The platypus (Ornithorhynchus anatinus) is a unique combination of reptile, bird and mammal.They inhabit freshwater rivers and lagoons from Tasmania to northern Queensland.

One of the real wonders of the animal world, the echidna has a long tongue coated with sticky fluid which it inserts into ant holes. When withdrawn, the tongue is covered with hundreds of ants.

The dingo does not bark like the ordinary dog but makes a sustained, dismal howl and that only at night. His ears are alwa erect, his tail is bushy and his canine teeth are usually longer th those of the domestic dog. Their colour varies but is normally a tawny yellow with paler belly, white tail tip and feet.

Dingoes are believed to have inhabited Australia for more than 10 000 years and have so far eluded man's attempt to conquer them. The wild dog, although eradicated from many of the southern pastoral districts, still has a wide territory in northern and central Australia.

uit bats form 'camps' consisting of thousands of individuals
o fly great distances in search for food, always returning to
ir home base.

ique to Australia, the Tasmanian devil (Sarcophilus harrisii) is
ancient marsupial predator. About a metre long, this stocky
eature is less ferocious than it looks. It is found in the isolated
hlands of Tasmania.

25

Camels running wild near the Olgas. Introduced from India in the nineteenth century, camels proved invaluable in the development of the arid interior of Australia for more than half a century. Displaced by motor transport, the few that remain mostly roam free.

Water buffaloes roaming free in the Northern Territory.

These sharp-toothed, small-eyed saurians have become a rather gruesome tourist attraction in the north of the continent. There are two species of crocodiles: the relatively harmless freshwater crocodile and the more lethal saltwater variety.

The tree-frogs of the Australian bush are noted for their night concerts when the air comes alive with a rich chorus of sound.

A banksia provides a resting place for a small native frog.▼

The taipan (Oxyuranus scutellatus) *is one of the most lethal in the world. Found in northern Queensland, it can grow to more than 3 metres and has fangs almost a centimetre long. The taipan carries an enormous quantity of venom—enough to kill 200 sheep.* ▲

A sandhill python basks in the sweltering heat near Ayers Rock. There are nine species of python in Australia. (Following page.)

Introduced into Queensland in the 1930s to combat the spread of the sugarcane beetles, the cane toad is now well established along Queensland's coastal regions and in north-eastern New South Wales.▼

The common red-bellied black snake is venomous but no fatalities have been recorded in adults. ◄

Confident of its ability to ward off attacks, the harmless thorny devil lizard (Moloch horridus) *basks openly in sand patches.*

The large lace lizard, or goanna, can grow as long as 2 metres. (Following page.)

The king brown snake, one of about 160 distinct species of snakes that are found in Australia. ◄

...e sand goanna (Perentie-varanus giganteus) *is found in ...orthern and central Australia and can grow as long ...2.4 metres.*

...e most spectacular of Australia's reptiles, the frilled lizard (...hlamydosaurus kingii) uses its amazing Elizabethan collar to ...uff attackers and as a storehouse for food. The insects it catches ...e kept in the folds of the collar until required. ◄

...he strange-looking bearded dragon lizard is a stoutly built ...llow up to 60 centimetres in length. He relies upon camouflage ...r protection, rarely running from danger. ►

The aggressive funnel-web spider is the most deadly spider in Australia. They spin a silken T-shaped funnel in their burrows and when cornered rear up with fangs opened ready to strike.

One of the most poisonous of Australia's spiders, the red-back has a body the size of a large pea and is a relative of the black widow spider of North America.

Very large and fast moving, the non-poisonous huntsman spider is often found inside homes and is commonly called a 'tarantula'.

The large red and grey kangaroos are well known to all Australians and around the world. A kangaroo appears on the nation's Coat of Arms and a Flying Kangaroo adorns the tail of all Qantas jets. Some kangaroos are extinct, some rare and some so common as to be pests. Most live on the ground but some live on cliffs and others in trees.

The smallest of the kangaroo family, the musky rat-kangaroo, is a miniature kangaroo and not related in the slightest to rats. It is an inhabitant of the rainforest floor around Cairns and weighs about 500 grams.

The hare-wallabies are kangaroos about the size of hares. Two species are extinct, two are very rare and the spectacled hare-wallaby is still found in the open country of northern Australia.

In appearance, much more like kangaroos 'should look' are the rock-wallabies. However, unlike the 'proper' kangaroos, rock-wallabies are more like goats in their habits.

Most suitable parts of the country, with the exception of Tasmania, have or had a local species of rock-wallaby. Many are distinctively marked and all are highly agile on steep rock faces. The yellow-footed rock-wallaby is brightly coloured and marked with yellow limbs and tail and prominent black and white patches. Its home is the arid rocky ranges of central South Australia, far western New South Wales and central Queensland. The more widespread black-footed rock-wallaby is a popular tourist attraction at Simpsons Gap National Park near Alice Springs.

A little-known group of kangaroos are the tree-kangaroos. Although centred on New Guinea two species occur in far northern Queensland. They live in rainforests and are well adapted to their tree-dwelling existence. Nobody could claim they were agile climbers; however, in their own way they are efficient at getting about in the trees. They also spend a considerable amount of time feeding on the ground.

The larger and typical kangaroos are variously known as wallabies, wallaroos and kangaroos. There are no strict differences except that the wallabies tend to be smaller and the kangaroos the larger species. The wallaroos fall somewhere in between.

Typical of the wallabies is the red-necked wallaby. Standing about 50 centimetres high and with a tail some 65 centimetres in length this is the common wallaby of the forests of south-eastern Australia. The neck has a rufous wash. The tips of the muzzle, toes, tail and paws are black. Otherwise this wallaby is generally grey.

The gestation period of the red-necked wallaby is about thirty days. The young will remain in the pouch for up to ten months. The female may become pregnant again while there is a youngster in the pouch but the gestation will be interrupted. The unborn young will not be born until the young living in the pouch leaves permanently. The unborn youngster may remain in a suspended state for almost a year. This adaptation is common among the kangaroos. It enables them to respond quickly to favourable weather conditions and is insurance against the loss of pouched young.

The big red and the blue flier

The largest of all the kangaroos is the red kangaroo. The male is usually brick-red in colour and the female, sometimes called the 'blue flier', is blue-grey. Large males can be quite massive. The total length from nose to tip of tail is up to 2.5 metres. Large males can weigh up to 85 kilograms.

Red kangaroos are found throughout arid Australia. Feeding is usually at night and although they do drink at stock troughs and dams, they can exist without water when on green food. Red kangaroos are able to modify their breeding patterns to suit the climatic conditions. During drought, breeding stops altogether and when conditions are flush, breeding is maximised. A female red kangaroo can have an out-of-pouch young still suckling on one teat, a pouched young living on another and an embryo in a suspended gestation in the uterus. Among the remarkable adaptations that enable this breeding pattern is the female's ability to produce different compositions of milk suitable for ages of the two young.

The red kangaroo and several other kangaroo species are the subject of a controversial culling and commercial-use programme. Large numbers of kangaroos can have a major impact on commercial agricultural production. A detailed system of assessing kangaroo numbers has been developed, and permits are given for property owners to remove fixed numbers of problem animals. Under strict regulation some of these animals are then allowed to be used commercially.

It is an emotionally charged issue. The animal welfare groups are strongly against the culling, arguing that the kangaroos are threatened, that the killing of the animals is cruel and that wildlife should not be exploited.

However, if the issues are examined carefully it will be seen that not only can a sustainable, humane kangaroo industry be maintained but that it is in the interests of nature conservation that it be allowed to continue.

In any discussion of kangaroo harvesting, it is important from the outset to define 'kangaroo'. As has been already discussed, the kangaroo family includes a large number of species, some common, some rare and some already extinct. 'Kangaroo' here refers to the three large commercially harvested species: the red kangaroo and the eastern grey and western grey kangaroos.

Large numbers of these species exist and are mainly concentrated in sheep country. Surveys early this decade indicated a total nation-wide kangaroo population at about 20 million animals. Drought can reduce these numbers by around 40 per cent. But this is the norm for kangaroos whose remarkable breeding biology is designed to take advantage of good seasons when they come. Even an annual harvest of several hundred thousands of animals fails to stop an increase in animals in good seasons. We now have good scientific data to demonstrate that annual harvesting of the three large kangaroo species is sustainable indefinitely. The historical facts support this. In the last fifty years over one million skins have been exported on average annually. There is no sign of decline in the kangaroo population.

Arguments of cruelty are not supported since within moments of being spotlighted, commercially harvested kangaroos are shot. This compares with the days of yarding, trucking and culling of sheep and cattle that are taken to an abattoir. Finally it seems irrational to try to draw a moral line between utilisation of kangaroos, or other wild animals, and domestic stock. Isn't the difference purely conceptual and how does that justify one and not the other?

A major deleterious effect of the campaigns against kangaroo harvesting is that it takes effort away from the important conservation issues. Many of the smaller kangaroos are endangered and need urgent attention. While we fight conceptual battles real animals are disappearing.

Despite the great diversity of the native animals the early settlers for various reasons felt a strong urge to introduce familiar animals from their old homelands. Sometimes, as is the case of releasing pigs and goats on remote islands, it was to ensure the survival of anyone becoming shipwrecked in the future. Sometimes, as with foxes and rabbits, it was to provide sport. In other situations animals were introduced as beasts of burden, hence the populations of wild camels and water buffaloes. Finally, many exotic animals such as black rats were accidentally introduced to their new homes.

Who could have believed that the humble European rabbit would be so successful and so destructive in its new home? First released in 1858 for sport shooting, the rabbit spread within sixty years to cover half the continent. Even with modern control techniques including poisons and myxomatosis the impact of rabbits on agricultural production and native animals is still high. Pigs, goats, cats and donkeys also have their economic and ecological impacts.

The stories of water buffaloes and camels in Australia have an ironic twist. Both species were introduced to Australia and both cause significant damage (very severe in the case of the buffalo). Australia has large wild populations of both these species and now exports animals back to their original homes. In the case of the camels the only wild animals anywhere in the world are in central Australia and small numbers are exported to Saudi Arabia.

The most widespread exotic animal and the one that may cause the greatest environmental damage is the feral cat. Descendant of domestic felines they are now truly wild animals. They are most active at night and feed on live animals up to the size of a brush-tailed possum. Unfortunately the feral cat is now well established from the rainforests to the desert.

Not all snakes are venomous. Despite man's instinctive fear of snakes there are many species of snakes that are quite harmless. These include the file snakes, blind snakes, tree snakes and others. The largest snakes in the country, the pythons, are also not venomous but very large specimens could be dangerous since they kill by constriction. Australia's largest snake is the Oenpelli python which can grow to over 6 metres.

However, it is the dangerous snakes that capture the attention of most people.

Venomous snakes

Until recently it was believed that the taipan of coastal Queensland and the Northern Territory was Australia's most deadly snake. It is found in a range of habitat types and feeds at night as well as during the day. Prior to 1955, when an antivenom became available, bites were invariably fatal and many deaths occurred. The taipan has been recorded at over 3 metres long and is very fast across the ground.

A snake which was first tested in 1975 has been found to be four times deadlier than the taipan. It is the small-scaled snake which fortunately is found only in arid sparsely settled country in central Australia. This snake is a thousand times more toxic than the diamondback rattlesnake of North America.

Another highly dangerous and distinctively shaped snake is the death adder. This species is found throughout mainland Australia and has an immediately recognisable 'viper' shape. This snake prefers to conceal itself in leaf litter or soil and leave its tail exposed beside its waiting mouth. As small animals wander by, it twitches its tail to lure them close for attack. Fortunately this snake, like most, rarely attacks humans unless deliberately provoked.

Sea-snakes are common in tropical waters and are highly dangerous. Most attacks occur when the snakes are being handled on a beach or when the snake is accidentally caught in fishing nets.

Australia's largest lizards are known locally as goannas. In Africa and Asia they are known as monitor lizards and include the world's largest lizard, the komodo dragon. The Australian bush is full of tall stories concerning long goannas. Goannas are supposed to relish the idea of escaping from danger by running up the bare legs of female pursuers! Also, if a goanna bites you, be warned that the wound will reopen on the seventh anniversary of the bite! As with many bush yarns, there is an element of truth in the stories.

When frightened, goannas run up the treetrunks or fence posts as a means of escape. Also, since goannas eat carrion, a bite will often become infected and keep reopening. None of Australia's goannas are dangerous unless they are forced to bite or scratch when cornered.

A large group of Australian lizards are known as dragons. Two members of the dragon group are quite unmistakeable. The thorny devil is a tiny desert-dweller which is covered in spiny scales. It is a slow-moving little lizard that hunts ants during daylight hours. It is an animal strongly associated with inland sand-dunes and could be a symbol for Alice Springs and the Red Centre. Preferring the wet tropics, the frilled lizard is a dragon which can reach a length of over 2 metres. This big lizard is usually encountered on the ground where it searches for insects and other small animals. When alarmed it faces the intruder and raises its frill which almost totally surrounds its head. This gives the lizard the appearance of great size and can deter a would-be predator. If a hurried retreat is required, the frilled lizard raises itself onto its back legs and makes for the nearest tree.

Skinks, geckos and legless lizards make up the rest of the lizard families.

The dangerous crocodile

The recent worldwide successes of the Australian film *Crocodile Dundee* starring Paul Hogan has thrown a previously little-known ancient Australian into the spotlight—the estuarine crocodile. Unfortunately this publicity has been fuelled by a number of recent fatal crocodile attacks. Few people realise that the estuarine crocodile is the most dangerous crocodile in the world and also one of the most dangerous animals in the world.

The estuarine crocodile is found throughout south-east Asia, Indonesia, New Guinea and the south-west Pacific. The most viable population, however, occurs in northern Australia, centred on the Northern Territory. The smaller Johnston's crocodile is found in the same areas but feeds entirely on fish.

Estuarine crocodiles give no warning of attack. The prey, usually wallabies or other small animals, is usually taken from the water's edge. The crocodile locates its prey and then approaches from under the water. In a surge of power the reptile launches up to several metres from the water and clasps the victim in its vicelike jaws. The crocodile then heads back to deep water where the victim is drowned. If the prey is large, the reptile may back into the water while rolling—the infamous death roll. This has the effect of stunning the victim and reducing its chances of escape.

When in crocodile country precautions should be taken to avoid attack. It would certainly be foolish to swim in waters known to contain estuarine (also unwisely known as saltwater) crocodiles. Estuarine crocodiles live much of their lives in fresh water many kilometres from the sea. It is also sensible not to be involved in any activities designed to attract wild crocodiles. Some unscrupulous tour operators feed wild crocodiles, which places not only their paying customers at risk, but also other river users. It is also good practice not to leave food scraps such as cleaned fish around boat ramps. This only encourages crocodiles to frequent places where fishermen and other boat users gather.

After years of uncontrolled hunting crocodiles were fully protected in Australia in about 1970. The numbers are now building up again. Careful plans are in place to keep cities, towns and properties clear of dangerous animals while at the same time guaranteeing the long-term survival of these remarkable relatives of the dinosaurs.

The inland rivers stock some of the most interesting and popular sports fish anywhere in the world. However, the total numbers of freshwater fish species are not large, owing to the dry nature of the continent.

The Queensland lungfish is a sluggish metre-long inhabitant of the coastal rivers of central Queensland. Unlike most fish, this predator breathes air from the surface of the water. The lungfish has gills as well as lungs.

Several species of eels frequent the coastal rivers as well. Typical of freshwater eels, breeding occurs in the ocean and very long migrations are undertaken for the young to return to the ancestral freshwater rivers.

Perhaps the most famous freshwater fish of inland waters of southern Australia is the giant Murray cod. Specimens have been recorded at 113 kilograms and today fish of about 30 kilograms are still regularly caught.

Breeding by Murray cod is triggered by rising floodwater in spring. Up to 40 000 eggs are laid among the debris on the bottom of the river. The adult fish feed mainly on other fish and shellfish.

The number of these Murray cod has declined over the years and this has been attributed to overfishing and the effects of introduced fish. The greatest likely factor is the controlling of the river flow by artificial dams.

Unfortunately, despite the good fishing to be had with our home-grown Australian fish, the lure of the Old Country has been too great for the fishing fraternity. English perch, rainbow trout and brown trout have been released into many Australian streams. Despite our experience with the devastating effects of the release of other foreign animals into the Australian environment government agencies still sponsor the release of exotic fish. Often the same government agencies are responsible for the control of other exotic species. It seems a strange paradox.

Among the invertebrate animals, the Australian continent is just as uniquely endowed as with the more advanced feathered and furred species.

Over fifty different species of termites, or white ants, are to be found here. A termite's mound is the home of a large number of infertile worker termites and a single pair of breeding adults. The social order is similar to that of a beehive with a single fertile queen.

Termites live on wood and underground tunnels are dug linking the mound with the food source. Where the mound is in a tree the tunnels are within the wood of the tree. Termite mounds are remarkable pieces of engineering. The outside layer of the mound is solid earth which insulates against high temperatures. In very hot climates, galleries are built in the outer layers of earth and filled with good insulating material such as stored food, waste products or lengths of grass. In addition the mounds are built in such a way that the hottest sun does not hit the mound directly. Convection currents are set up which draw cooling air through the mound; a termite-designed air-conditioning system! The central living galleries of the mound are thereby maintained at a constant temperature.

Deadly spiders

In addition to many unique spiders, Australia has the dubious honour of being home to the most dangerous spider in the world.

It is the Sydney funnel-web and male spiders have caused deaths in children in less than two hours. Fortunately the spider is large and relatively easy to distinguish. An antivenom became available for bites of this funnel-web spider in 1980. In the past it was usually children, elderly people or pregnant women that were most at risk from the bites of this spider.

Red-back spiders are found throughout Australia and are also highly dangerous. Deaths have occurred from bites of this spider; however, no fatalities have been recorded since antivenom became available in 1956. The female spider is highly distinctive, possessing a bright red spot on the black body. The Australian red-back spider is a close relative of the dangerous black widow spider of North America and the katipo of New Zealand.

Index

Numbers in *italics* denote colour photographs.

Acknowledgements

Australian Picture Library/ZEFA: page 15.
Douglass Baglin: pages 16–17 below, 18, 20.
John Carnemolla: pages 16–17 above, 20 above, 22, 25, 26, 36–7.
Dallas and John Heaton: pages 10 below, 11, 12, 13.
Raymond Hosier: page 30 below.
Alan Jones: page 14.
Gary Lewis: pages 10 above, 17 above, 19, 20 below, 28, 29, 39 below.
Fritz Prenzel: pages 17 below, 31.
Derek Roff: pages 21, 23, 24, 26, 30 above, 32–3, 34, 39 above.